GW00339246

easy meals

Vegetarian

p

This is a Parragon Book
First printed in 2001

Parragon
Queen Street House
4 Queen Street
Bath BA1 1HE
United Kingdom

ISBN: 0-75255-768-8

Printed in Spain

Produced by The Bridgewater Book Company Ltd, Lewes, East Sussex

Creative Director Terry Jeavons
Art Director Sarah Howerd
Page Make-up Sara Kidd
Editorial Director Fiona Biggs
Senior Editor Mark Truman
Editorial Assistant Tom Kitch

NOTES FOR THE READER

- This book uses both metric and imperial measurements. Follow the same units of measurement throughout; do not mix metric and imperial.
- All spoon measurements are level: teaspoons and assumed to be 5 ml, and tablespoons are assumed to be 15 ml.
- Unless otherwise stated, milk is assumed to be full-fat, eggs and individual vegetables such as potatoes are medium-sized, and pepper is freshly ground black pepper.
- Recipes using raw or very lightly cooked eggs should be avoided by infants, the elderly, pregnant women, convalescents, and anyone suffering from an illness.
- Optional ingredients, variations and serving suggestions have not been included in the calculations. The times given are an approximate guide only. Preparation times differ according to the techniques used by different people and the cooking times vary as a result of the type of oven used.

Contents

Introduction

A vegetarian diet needs planning to ensure that it includes all the essential nutrients. If you are a vegetarian and often find yourself short of time to plan a meal, you may habitually fall back on fast foods which do not make up a balanced diet. The cheese and tomato sandwich you have for lunch may look completely different from the cheese and tomato pizza you have for supper, but they have essentially the same nutritional value.

The recipes in the following pages have been chosen to ensure that your meals are not only nutritious and simple to prepare for a quick lunch or supper, but that they are also inspiring. The recipes include plenty of protein in the form of a wide range of beans and pulses, nuts, and grains such as rice, barley, and wheat, vitamins, minerals and calcium from many different sources, plus rich and exotic flavourings from herbs and spices.

guide to recipe key	
easy	Recipes are graded as follows: 1 pea = easy; 2 peas = very easy; 3 peas = extremely easy.
serves 4	Most of the recipes in this book serve four people. Simply halve the ingredients to serve two, taking care not to mix imperial and metric measurements.
15 minutes	Preparation time. Where recipes include marinating, soaking, standing, or chilling, times for these are listed separately: eg, 15 minutes, plus 30 minutes to marinate.
15 minutes	Cooking time. Cooking times do not include the cooking of rice or noodles served with the main dishes.

This wide variety of ingredients is the basis for a rich store of new ideas for dishes which are all easy to cook.

The recipes come from all over the world, so there is plenty of scope for creating interesting menus. A smooth vegetable soup followed by Spicy Cashew Nut Curry, or Vegetable Tostadas served with a salad of mixed greens is one flavoursome example. And guests will be impressed by a classic Greek salad followed by colourful Red Rice Pilaf with Roasted Vegetables and Almond Rice Custard or Chocolate Hazelnut Pots to finish.

Aubergine & Mushroom-stuffed Omelette, page 44

Soups & Starters

Several of the soups and starters in this section also work well as light lunch or supper dishes – Barley & Rice Soup with Chard is so packed with goodness, it's a meal in itself. Hummus, too – a delicious dip made from chickpeas and tahini (crushed sesame seeds), flavoured with garlic, olive oil and lemon – is a great dish, full of protein and calcium, and a perfect snack served with pitta bread and a selection of crisp, raw vegetables.

Spinach Soup

INGREDIENTS

1 tbsp olive oil
1 onion, halved and
    thinly sliced
1 leek, split lengthways
    and thinly sliced
1 potato, finely diced
1 litre/1¾ pints water
2 sprigs fresh marjoram
    or ¼ tsp dried
2 sprigs fresh thyme or
    ¼ tsp dried
1 bay leaf
400 g/14 oz young
    spinach, washed
freshly grated nutmeg
salt and pepper
4 tbsp single cream,
    to serve

❶ Heat the oil in a heavy-based saucepan over a medium heat. Add the onion and leek and cook for about 3 minutes, stirring occasionally, until they begin to soften.

❷ Add the potato, water, marjoram, thyme and bay leaf, along with a pinch of salt. Bring to the boil, reduce the heat, cover and cook gently for about 25 minutes, or until the vegetables are tender. Remove the bay leaf and herb stems.

❸ Add the spinach and continue cooking for 3–4 minutes, stirring frequently, just until it is completely wilted.

❹ Allow the soup to cool slightly, then transfer to a blender or food processor and purée until smooth, working in batches if necessary. (If using a food processor, strain off the cooking liquid and reserve. Purée the soup solids with enough cooking liquid to moisten them, then combine with the remaining liquid.)

❺ Return the soup to the saucepan and thin with a little more water, if wished. Season with salt, a good grinding of pepper and a generous grating of nutmeg. Place over a low heat and simmer until reheated.

❻ Ladle the soup into warm bowls and swirl a tablespoonful of cream into each serving.

 very easy

serves 4

15 minutes

45 minutes

Roasted Pumpkin & Tomato Soup

INGREDIENTS

1–2 tbsp olive oil
900 g/2 lb peeled
  pumpkin flesh, cut
  into slices 2 cm/
  ¾ inch thick
450 g/1 lb ripe tomatoes,
  skinned, cored and
  thickly sliced
1 onion, chopped finely
2 garlic cloves, chopped
  finely
4 tbsp white wine
2 tbsp water
600 ml/1 pint vegetable
  stock
125 ml/4 fl oz single
  cream
salt and pepper
snipped chives,
  to garnish

❶ Drizzle 1 tablespoon of the olive oil over the base of a large baking dish. Lay the pumpkin, tomatoes, onion and garlic in the dish in 2 or 3 layers. Drizzle the remaining olive oil over the top, then pour over the wine and water. Season with a little salt and pepper.

❷ Cover with kitchen foil and bake in a preheated oven at 190°C/375°F/Gas Mark 5 for about 45 minutes, or until all the vegetables are soft.

❸ Allow the vegetables to cool slightly, then transfer to a blender or a food processor and add the cooking juices and as much stock as is needed to cover the vegetables. Blend until smooth, working in batches if necessary.

❹ Pour the purée into a saucepan and stir in the remaining stock. Cook gently over a medium heat, stirring occasionally, for about 15 minutes, or until heated through. Stir in the cream and continue cooking for 3–4 minutes.

❺ Taste and adjust the seasoning, if necessary. Ladle the soup into warm bowls, garnish with chives, and serve.

very easy

serves 4

25 minutes

1 hour 5 minutes

Soup of Beans & Greens

INGREDIENTS

250 g/9 oz dried haricot
  or cannellini beans
1 tbsp olive oil
2 onions, chopped finely
4 garlic cloves, chopped
  finely
1 celery stick, sliced
  thinly
2 carrots, halved and
  sliced thinly
1.2 litres/2 pints water
¼ tsp dried thyme
¼ tsp dried marjoram
1 bay leaf
125 g/4½ oz leafy greens,
  such as chard,
  mustard, spinach and
  kale, washed
salt and pepper

❶ Pick over the beans, cover with cold water, and leave to soak for 6 hours or overnight. Drain the beans, put them in a saucepan, and add cold water to cover by 5 cm/2 inches. Bring to the boil, simmer for 10 minutes. Drain and rinse.

❷ Heat the oil in a saucepan, add the onion, and cook, covered, for 3–4 minutes, stirring, until just softened. Add the garlic, celery and carrots, and cook for 2 minutes.

❸ Add the water, beans, thyme, marjoram and bay leaf. When the mixture bubbles, reduce the heat. Cover and simmer, stirring occasionally, for 1¼ hours or until the beans are tender. Season to taste.

❹ Allow the soup to cool slightly, then transfer 450 ml/ 16 fl oz to a blender or a food processor. Blend until smooth and recombine with the soup.

❺ Cut the greens, a handful at a time, into thin ribbons, cutting on the diagonal. Keep spinach and other thin leaves separate, but add the thicker leaves to the soup and cook gently, uncovered, for 10 minutes. Stir in the thinner greens and cook for 5–10 minutes, or until tender.

❻ Taste and adjust the seasoning, if necessary. Ladle the soup into warm bowls, and serve.

easy

serves 4

15 minutes

2 hours

Barley & Rice Soup with Chard

INGREDIENTS

100 g/3½ oz pearl barley
100 g/3½ oz long-grain brown rice
450 g/1 lb chard, trimmed and soaked for 10 minutes
2 tbsp olive oil
1 large onion, chopped finely
2 carrots, chopped finely
2 celery sticks, chopped finely
2 garlic cloves, chopped finely
400 g/14 oz canned chopped Italian plum tomatoes with their juice
1 bay leaf
1 tsp dried thyme
1 tsp herbes de Provence or dried oregano
1 litre/1¾ pints vegetable stock
450 g/1 lb canned cannellini beans, drained
2 tbsp chopped fresh parsley
salt and pepper
freshly grated Parmesan cheese, to serve

❶ Bring a large saucepan of water to the boil. Add the barley and the brown rice, and return to the boil. Reduce the heat and simmer gently for 30–35 minutes, or until just tender. Drain and set aside.

❷ Drain the chard. Cut out the hard white stems and slice the stems, cutting on the diagonal, into very thin strips; set aside. Roll the leaves into a long cigar shape and shred thinly; set aside.

❸ Heat the oil in a large saucepan. Add the onion, carrots and celery, and cook, stirring frequently, for about 5 minutes or until soft and beginning to colour. Add the garlic and cook for a minute longer. Add the tomatoes and their juice, the bay leaf, thyme and herbes de Provence. Reduce the heat and simmer, partially covered, for about 7 minutes, or until all the vegetables are soft.

❹ Stir in the sliced white chard stems and the stock. Simmer gently for about 20 minutes. Add the shredded green chard and simmer for a further 15 minutes.

❺ Stir in the beans and parsley with the cooked barley and brown rice. Season with salt and pepper. Bring back to the boil and simmer for a further 8–10 minutes. Serve immediately, with Parmesan cheese for sprinkling.

very easy

serves 4

15 minutes

1½ hours

Mexican Vegetable Soup with Tortilla Chips

INGREDIENTS

2 tbsp vegetable or
extra-virgin olive oil
1 onion, chopped finely
4 garlic cloves, chopped
finely
$\frac{1}{4}$–$\frac{1}{2}$ tsp ground cumin
2–3 tsp mild chilli
powder
1 carrot, sliced
1 waxy potato, diced
350 g/12 oz diced fresh
or canned tomatoes
1 courgette, diced
$\frac{1}{4}$ small cabbage,
shredded
1 litre/1$\frac{3}{4}$ pints vegetable
stock or water
1 corn-on-the-cob, the
kernels cut off the cob,
or 225 g/8 oz canned
sweetcorn
about 10 green or runner
beans, topped and
tailed, then cut into
bite-sized lengths
salt and pepper

TO SERVE
4–6 tbsp chopped fresh
coriander
salsa of your choice, or
chopped fresh chilli,
to taste
tortilla chips

very easy

serves 4

25 minutes

35 minutes

❶ Heat the oil in a heavy-based pan. Add the onion and garlic and cook for a few minutes until softened, then sprinkle in the cumin and chilli powder. Stir in the carrot, potato, tomatoes, courgettes and cabbage, and cook for 2 minutes, stirring the mixture occasionally.

❷ Pour in the stock. Cover and cook over a medium heat for about 20 minutes, or until the vegetables are tender.

❸ Add extra water if necessary, then stir in the sweetcorn and green beans and cook for a further 5–10 minutes, or until the beans are tender. Season with salt and pepper to taste, bearing in mind that the tortilla chips may be salty.

❹ Ladle the soup into soup bowls and sprinkle each portion with fresh coriander. Top with a dab of salsa, then add a handful of tortilla chips.

16

Hummus

INGREDIENTS

200 g/7 oz dried
   chickpeas
2 large garlic cloves
7 tbsp extra-virgin olive
   oil
2½ tbsp tahini
1 tbsp lemon juice, or
   to taste
salt and pepper

TO GARNISH
extra-virgin olive oil
paprika
fresh coriander

❶ Place the chickpeas in a large bowl. Pour in at least twice the volume of cold water to beans and leave to stand for at least 12 hours, or until they double in size.

❷ Drain the chickpeas. Put them in a large flameproof casserole or a saucepan and add twice the volume of water to beans. Bring to the boil and boil hard for 10 minutes, skimming the surface.

❸ Lower the heat and leave to simmer for 1 hour, skimming the surface if necessary, or until the chickpeas are tender. Meanwhile, cut the garlic cloves in half, remove the pale green or white cores, and chop roughly. Set aside.

❹ Drain the chickpeas, reserving 4 tablespoons of the cooking liquid. Put the olive oil, garlic, tahini and lemon juice in a food processor and blend to a smooth paste.

❺ Add the chickpeas and pulse until they are finely ground but the hummus is still lightly textured. Add a little of the reserved cooking liquid if the mixture is too thick. Season with salt and pepper to taste.

❻Transfer to a bowl, cover with clingfilm, and chill until ready to serve. To serve, drizzle with olive oil and sprinkle with a little paprika, and garnish with fresh coriander.

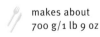 very easy

makes about
700 g/1 lb 9 oz

10 minutes

1½ hours, plus
12 hours to soak

Aubergine Spread

INGREDIENTS

2 large aubergines
1 tomato
1 garlic clove, chopped
4 tbsp extra-virgin
   olive oil
2 tbsp lemon juice
2 tbsp pine kernels,
   lightly toasted
2 spring onions,
   chopped finely
salt and pepper

TO GARNISH
ground cumin
2 tbsp chopped finely
fresh flat-leaved parsley

❶ Using a fork or a metal skewer, pierce the aubergines all over. Place them on a baking sheet in a preheated oven at 230°C/450°F/Gas Mark 8 and roast for 20–25 minutes, or until they are very soft.

❷ Use a folded tea towel to remove the aubergines from the baking sheet, and set them aside to cool.

❸ Place the tomato in a heatproof bowl, pour boiling water over to cover it, and leave it to stand for 30 seconds. Drain, then plunge it into cold water to prevent it from cooking. Skin the tomato, then cut it in half and scoop out the seeds with a teaspoon. Dice the flesh finely, and set it aside.

❹ Cut the aubergines in half lengthways. Scoop out the flesh with a spoon and transfer it to a food processor. Add the garlic, olive oil, lemon juice, pine kernels, and salt and pepper to taste. Process until smooth.

❺ Spoon the mixture into a bowl and stir in the spring onions and diced tomato. Cover and chill for 30 minutes before serving.

❻ Garnish the dip with a pinch of ground cumin and the chopped parsley, then serve.

 very easy

 makes about 400 g/14 oz

 15 minutes

 20–25 minutes, plus 30 minutes to chill

Greek Salad

INGREDIENTS

250 g/9 oz feta cheese
250 g/9 oz cucumber
250 g/9 oz Greek
   kalamata olives
1 red onion or 4 spring
   onions
2 large juicy tomatoes
1 tsp honey
4 tbsp extra-virgin
   olive oil
½ lemon
salt and pepper
fresh or dried oregano,
   to garnish
pitta bread, to serve

❶ Drain the feta cheese if it is packed in brine. Place it on a chopping board and cut into 1 cm/½ inch dice. Transfer to a salad bowl.

❷ Cut the cucumber in half lengthways and use a teaspoon to scoop out the seeds. Cut the flesh into 1 cm/½ inch slices. Add to the bowl with the feta cheese.

❸ Stone the olives with an olive or cherry pitter and add them to the salad bowl. Slice the red onion or chop the white and green parts of the spring onions finely, and add them to the salad bowl.

❹ Cut each tomato into quarters and scoop out the seeds with a teaspoon. Cut the flesh into bite-sized pieces and add to the bowl.

extremely easy

serves 4

30 minutes

0 minutes

❺ Using your hands, toss all the ingredients gently together. Stir the honey into the olive oil (see Cook's Tip), add to the salad, and squeeze in lemon juice to taste. Season to taste with pepper and a little salt. Cover and chill until required.

❻ Garnish with the oregano and serve with pitta bread.

COOK'S TIP
The small amount of honey helps to bring out the full flavour of the tomatoes.

Sweet Potato Cakes with Soy & Tomato Sauce

INGREDIENTS

2 sweet potatoes, 500 g/
1 lb 2 oz total weight
2 garlic cloves, crushed
1 small green chilli,
chopped
2 sprigs coriander,
chopped
1 tbsp dark soy sauce
plain flour for shaping
vegetable oil for frying
sesame seeds for
sprinkling

SOY & TOMATO SAUCE
2 tsp vegetable oil
1 garlic clove, chopped
finely
2 cm/³⁄₄ inch piece fresh
ginger root, chopped
finely
3 tomatoes, skinned and
chopped
2 tbsp dark soy sauce
1 tbsp lime juice
2 tbsp fresh coriander,
chopped

❶ Mix the Soy & Tomato Sauce ingredients together in a bowl. Heat the oil in a wok and stir-fry the garlic and ginger for about 1 minute. Add the tomatoes and stir-fry for another 2 minutes. Remove from the heat and stir in the soy sauce, lime and coriander. Set aside and keep warm.

❷ Peel the sweet potatoes and grate finely (you can do this quickly with a food processor). Place the garlic, chilli and coriander in a pestle and mortar and crush to a smooth paste. Stir in the soy sauce mix with the sweet potatoes.

❸ Divide the mixture into 12 equal portions. Dip into flour and pat into a flat, round patty shape.

❹ Heat a shallow layer of oil in a wide frying pan. Fry the sweet potato patties over a high heat until golden, turning once.

❺ Drain on kitchen paper and sprinkle with sesame seeds. Serve hot, with a spoonful of the Soy & Tomato Sauce.

easy

serves 4

25 minutes

20 minutes

Main Meals

Cultures that are not predominantly vegetarian often come up with some of the most tempting meat-free dishes. A perfect example of this is Spanakopittas, a delicious crisp pastry stuffed with spinach and feta cheese, sold in generous slices in Greek bakeries throughout the day; while a basic Italian risotto can be dressed up with different vegetables and cheeses to make an elegant but very satisfying vegetarian meal – try Wild Rocket & Tomato Risotto with Mozzarella.

Vegetable Chilli

INGREDIENTS

1 medium aubergine,
   peeled if wished, cut
   into 2.5 cm/1 inch
   slices
1 tbsp olive oil, plus extra
   for brushing
1 large red or yellow
   onion, chopped finely
2 peppers, chopped
   finely
3–4 garlic cloves,
   chopped finely or
   crushed
800 g/28 oz canned
   chopped tomatoes
   in juice
1 tbsp mild chilli powder,
   or to taste
½ tsp ground cumin
½ tsp dried oregano
2 small courgettes,
   quartered lengthways
   and sliced
400 g/14 oz canned
   kidney beans, drained
   and rinsed
450 ml/16 fl oz water
1 tbsp tomato purée
6 spring onions,
   chopped finely
115 g/4 oz grated
   Cheddar cheese
salt and pepper

❶ Brush the aubergine slices on one side with olive oil. Heat half the oil in a large frying pan over a medium-high heat. Add the aubergine, oiled side up, and cook for 5–6 minutes, or until browned on one side. Turn, brown the other side, and transfer to a plate. Cut into bite-sized pieces.

❷ Heat the remaining oil in a large saucepan over a medium heat. Add the onion and peppers, cover, and cook for 3–4 minutes, stirring occasionally, until the onion is just softened. Add the garlic and continue cooking for 2–3 minutes, or until the onion begins to colour.

❸ Add the tomatoes, chilli powder, cumin and oregano. Season with salt and pepper. Bring just to the boil, reduce the heat, cover, and simmer for 15 minutes.

❹ Add the courgettes, aubergine pieces and beans. Stir in the water and tomato purée. Cover again and continue simmering for about 45 minutes, or until the vegetables are tender. Taste and adjust the seasoning. If you prefer it hotter, stir in a little more chilli powder.

❺ Season to taste. Ladle into bowls, and top with spring onions and cheese.

 very easy

 serves 4

 15 minutes

🕐 1½ hours

Spanakopittas

2 tbsp olive oil
6 spring onions,
  chopped
250 g/9 oz fresh young
  spinach leaves, tough
  stalks removed, rinsed
60 g/2¼ oz long-grain
  rice (not basmati),
  boiled until tender and
  drained
4 tbsp chopped fresh dill
4 tbsp chopped fresh
  parsley
4 tbsp pine kernels
2 tbsp raisins
60 g/2¼ oz feta cheese,
  drained if necessary
  and crumbled
1 nutmeg
pinch of cayenne pepper
  (optional)
40 sheets filo pastry
about 250 g/9 oz melted
  butter
pepper

❶ Heat the oil in a pan, add the spring onions and fry for about 2 minutes. Add the spinach with the water clinging to the leaves, and cook, stirring, until the leaves wilt. Transfer to a bowl and, when cool enough to handle, squeeze dry.

❷ Stir in the rice, herbs, pine kernels, raisins and feta cheese. Grate in a-quarter of the nutmeg, and add black and cayenne peppers to taste.

❸ Leave the filo sheets in a stack. Cut forty 15 cm/6 inch squares. Remove 8 slices and cut into eight 10 cm/4 inch rounds. Re-wrap the unused pastry and cover the squares and rounds with a damp tea towel.

❹ Brush a 10 cm/4 inch tart tin with a removable base with butter. Put in one square of filo and brush with more butter. Repeat with 7 more sheets.

❺ Spoon in a quarter of the filling, top with a filo round and brush with butter. Repeat with another round. Fold the overhanging filo over the top and brush with butter.

❻ Make 3 more pies, then put the 4 pies on a baking sheet and bake in a preheated oven at 180°C/350°F/Gas Mark 4 for 20–25 minutes, or until crisp and golden. Leave to stand for 5 minutes before turning out.

easy

serves 4

20 minutes

30 minutes

Baked Aubergine Gratin

INGREDIENTS

1 large aubergine, about
  800 g/1 lb 12 oz
salt
300 g/10½ oz mozzarella
  cheese
85 g/3 oz Parmesan
  cheese
olive oil
250 ml/9 fl oz good-
  quality bottled tomato
  sauce for pasta
salt and pepper

❶ Top and tail the aubergine and cut into 5 mm/¼ inch slices crossways. Arrange the slices on a large plate, sprinkle with salt, and set aside for 30 minutes to drain.

❷ Meanwhile, drain and grate the mozzarella cheese and grate the Parmesan cheese finely. Set aside.

❸ Rinse the aubergine slices and pat dry with kitchen paper. Brush a baking sheet lightly with olive oil and arrange the aubergine slices in one layer. Brush with olive oil.

❹ Roast in a preheated oven at 200°C/400°F/Gas Mark 6 for 5 minutes. Using tongs, turn the slices and brush with a little oil, then bake for 5 minutes more, or until the aubergine is cooked through. Do not turn off the oven.

❺ Spread about 1 tablespoon olive oil over the bottom of a gratin dish or other ovenproof serving dish. Add a layer of aubergine slices, then a quarter of the tomato sauce, and top with a quarter of the mozzarella. Season to taste with salt and pepper.

❻ Continue layering until all the ingredients are used, ending with a layer of sauce. Sprinkle the Parmesan cheese over the top. Bake in the oven for 30 minutes, or until bubbling. Leave to stand for 5 minutes before serving.

 very easy

serves 4

20 minutes, plus
30 minutes to
drain

35 minutes

COOK'S TIP
Serve plenty of French bread with this dish because it produces the most delicious juices.

Spiced Lentils with Spinach

2 tbsp olive oil
1 large onion, chopped finely
1 large garlic clove, crushed
½ tbsp ground cumin
½ tsp ground ginger
250 g/9 oz Puy lentils
about 600 ml/1 pint vegetable stock
100 g/3½ oz baby spinach leaves
2 tbsp fresh mint leaves
1 tbsp fresh coriander leaves
1 tbsp fresh flat-leaved parsley leaves
freshly squeezed lemon juice
salt and pepper
grated lemon rind, to garnish

❶ Heat the olive oil in a large frying pan over a medium–high heat. Add the onion and cook for about 6 minutes. Stir in the garlic, cumin and ginger, and continue cooking, stirring occasionally, until the onion just starts to brown.

❷ Stir in the lentils. Pour in enough stock to cover the lentils by 2.5 cm/1 inch and bring to the boil. Lower the heat and simmer for 20 minutes, or according to the instructions on the packet, until the lentils are tender.

❸ Meanwhile, rinse the spinach leaves in several changes of cold water and shake dry. Finely chop the mint, coriander and parsley leaves.

❹ If there is no stock left in the pan, add a little extra. Add the spinach and stir in until it just wilts. Stir in the mint, coriander and parsley. Adjust the seasoning, adding lemon juice and salt and pepper. Transfer to a serving bowl and serve, garnished with lemon rind.

 very easy

 serves 4

10 minutes

 45 minutes

Hot & Sour Noodles

250 g/9 oz dried medium
  egg noodles
1 tbsp sesame oil
1 tbsp chilli oil
1 garlic clove, crushed
2 spring onions,
  chopped finely
55 g/2 oz button
  mushrooms, sliced
40 g/1½ oz dried Chinese
  black mushrooms,
  soaked, drained and
  sliced
2 tbsp lime juice
3 tbsp light soy sauce
1 tsp sugar

TO SERVE
shredded Chinese leaves
2 tbsp shredded
  coriander
2 tbsp toasted peanuts,
  chopped

❶ Cook the noodles in a pan of boiling water for 3–4 minutes, or according to the package directions. Drain well, return to the pan, toss with the sesame oil, and set aside.

❷ Heat the chilli oil in a large frying pan or wok and quickly stir-fry the garlic, onions and button mushrooms to soften them.

❸ Add the black mushrooms, lime juice, soy sauce and sugar, and continue stir-frying until boiling. Add the noodles and toss to mix.

❹ Serve spooned over Chinese leaves, sprinkled with coriander and peanuts.

 extremely easy

 serves 4

 15 minutes

 10 minutes

Mixed Vegetables in Peanut Sauce

INGREDIENTS

2 carrots, peeled
1 small head cauliflower, trimmed
2 small heads green pak choi
150 g/5½ oz French beans, topped and tailed, if wished
2 tbsp vegetable oil
1 garlic clove, chopped finely
6 spring onions, sliced
1 tsp chilli paste
2 tbsp soy sauce
2 tbsp rice wine
4 tbsp smooth peanut butter
3 tbsp coconut milk

 extremely easy

 serves 4

 20 minutes

 8–10 minutes

❶ Cut the carrots diagonally into thin slices. Cut the cauliflower into small florets, then slice the stalk thinly. Thickly slice the pak choi. Cut the beans into 3 cm/1¼ inch lengths.

❷ Heat the oil in a large frying pan or wok and stir-fry the garlic and spring onions for about 1 minute. Stir in the chilli paste and cook for a few seconds.

❸ Add the carrots and cauliflower and stir-fry for 2–3 minutes.

❹ Add the pak choi and beans and stir-fry for a further 2 minutes. Stir in the soy sauce and rice wine.

❺ Mix the peanut butter with the coconut milk and stir into the pan, then cook, stirring, for another minute. Serve immediately while still hot.

COOK'S TIP

It's important to cut the vegetables thinly into even-sized pieces so that they cook quickly and evenly. Prepare all the vegetables before you start to cook.

Oriental Vegetables with Yellow Bean Sauce

INGREDIENTS

1 aubergine
salt
2 tbsp vegetable oil
3 garlic cloves, crushed
4 spring onions,
   chopped
1 small red pepper,
   deseeded and sliced
   thinly
4 baby sweetcorn,
   halved lengthways
85 g/3 oz mangetouts
200 g/7 oz Chinese
   mustard greens,
   shredded roughly
425 g/15 oz canned
   Chinese straw
   mushrooms, drained
125 g/4½ oz beansprouts
2 tbsp rice wine
2 tbsp yellow bean sauce
2 tbsp dark soy sauce
1 tsp chilli sauce
1 tsp sugar
125 ml/4 fl oz vegetable
   stock
1 tsp cornflour
2 tsp water

❶ Trim the aubergine and cut into 5 cm/2 inch long matchsticks. Place in a colander, sprinkle with salt, and leave to drain for 30 minutes. Rinse in cold water and dry with kitchen paper.

❷ Heat the oil in a frying pan or wok and stir-fry the garlic, spring onions and pepper over a high heat for 1 minute. Stir in the aubergine pieces and stir-fry for another minute, or until softened.

❸ Stir in the sweetcorn and mangetouts and stir-fry for about 1 minute. Add the mustard greens, mushrooms and beansprouts, and stir-fry for 30 seconds.

❹ Mix together the rice wine, yellow bean sauce, soy sauce, chilli sauce and sugar, and add to the pan with the stock. Bring to the boil, stirring.

❺ Slowly blend the cornflour with the water to form a smooth paste. Stir quickly into the pan or wok and cook for a further minute. Serve immediately.

 very easy

 serves 4

15 minutes

10 minutes

Spiced Cashew Nut Curry

INGREDIENTS

250 g/9 oz unsalted
    cashew nuts
1 tsp coriander seeds
1 tsp cumin seeds
2 cardamom pods, crushed
1 tbsp sunflower oil
1 onion, sliced finely
1 garlic clove, crushed
1 small green chilli,
    deseeded and chopped
1 cinnamon stick
½ tsp ground turmeric
4 tbsp coconut cream
300 ml/10 fl oz hot
    vegetable stock
3 kaffir lime leaves,
    finely shredded
salt and pepper
boiled jasmine rice,
    to serve

 extremely easy

 serves 4

 10 minutes

 35 minutes

❶ Soak the cashew nuts in cold water overnight. Drain thoroughly. Crush the coriander, cumin seeds and cardamom pods in a pestle and mortar.

❷ Heat the oil and stir-fry the onion and garlic for 2–3 minutes to soften, but not brown. Add the chilli, crushed spices, cinnamon stick and turmeric, and stir-fry for another minute.

❸ Add the coconut cream and the hot stock to the pan. Bring to the boil, then add the cashew nuts and lime leaves.

❹ Cover the pan, lower the heat, and simmer for about 20 minutes. Serve hot, accompanied by jasmine rice.

COOK'S TIP

All spices give the best flavour when freshly crushed, but if you prefer, you can use ground spices instead of crushing them yourself in a pestle and mortar.

Aubergine & Mushroom-stuffed Omelette

3 tbsp vegetable oil
1 garlic clove, chopped
    finely
1 small onion, chopped
    finely
1 small aubergine, diced
½ small green pepper,
    deseeded and chopped
1 large dried Chinese
    black mushroom,
    soaked, drained and
    sliced
1 tomato, diced
1 tbsp light soy sauce
½ tsp sugar
¼ tsp ground black pepper
2 large eggs
salad leaves, tomato
    wedges and cucumber
    slices, to garnish

 very easy

 serves 4

 15 minutes

 10 minutes

❶ Heat half the oil and fry the garlic over a high heat for 30 seconds. Add the onion and the aubergine and continue to stir-fry until golden.

❷ Add the green pepper and stir-fry for a further minute to soften. Stir in the mushroom, tomato, soy sauce, sugar and pepper. Remove from the pan and keep hot.

❸ Beat the eggs together lightly. Heat the remaining oil, swirling to coat a wide area. Pour in the egg and swirl to set around the pan.

❹ When the egg is set, spoon the filling into the centre. Fold in the sides of the omelette to make a square parcel.

❺ Slide the omelette carefully onto a warmed dish and garnish with salad leaves, tomato wedges and cucumber slices. Serve hot.

COOK'S TIP
If you heat the pan thoroughly before adding the oil, and heat the oil before adding the ingredients, you should not have a problem with ingredients sticking to the pan.

Crispy Tofu with Chilli & Soy Sauce

INGREDIENTS

300 g/10½ oz firm tofu
2 tbsp vegetable oil
1 garlic clove, sliced
1 carrot, cut into
    matchsticks
½ green pepper,
    deseeded and cut
    into matchsticks
1 red bird-eye chilli,
    deseeded and
    chopped finely
2 tbsp soy sauce
1 tbsp lime juice
1 tbsp Thai fish sauce
1 tbsp soft light brown
    sugar
pickled garlic slices,
    to serve (optional)

❶ Drain the tofu and pat dry with kitchen paper. Cut into 2 cm/¾ inch cubes.

❷ Heat the oil in a wok and stir-fry the garlic for 1 minute. Remove the garlic and add the tofu, then fry quickly until well browned, turning gently to brown on all sides.

❸ Lift out the tofu, drain well and keep hot. Stir the carrot and pepper into the wok and stir-fry for 1 minute.

❹ Spoon the carrot and peppers onto a dish and pile the tofu on top.

❺ Mix together the chilli, soy sauce, lime juice, fish sauce and sugar, stirring until the sugar is dissolved.

❻ Spoon the same over the tofu and serve, perhaps topped with slices of pickled garlic. Serve hot.

extremely easy

serves 4

10 minutes

5–10 minutes

COOK'S TIP
Make sure to buy firm fresh tofu for this dish – the softer 'silken' type is more like junket in texture and not firm enough to hold its shape well during frying. It is better for adding to soups.

46

Refried Beans

500 g/1 lb 2 oz dried
   pinto or borlotti beans
spring each of mint,
   thyme and parsley
1 onion, cut into chunks
125 ml/4 fl oz vegetable
   oil or 125 g/4½ oz
   shortening or dripping
1–2 onions, chopped
½ tsp ground cumin
salt
250 g/9 oz grated
   Cheddar cheese
   (optional)

❶ Soak the beans overnight. Drain, place in a pan and cover with water and the herbs. Bring to the boil, then reduce the heat and simmer, covered, for 2 hours, or until the beans are tender. Add the onion and cook until the onion and beans are very tender. Put two-thirds of the cooked beans, with their cooking liquid, in a food processor and process to a purée. Stir in the remaining whole beans. Set aside.

❷ Heat the oil or fat in a frying pan. Add the onions and cook until very soft. Sprinkle with cumin and salt to taste.

❸ Ladle in a cupful of the bean mixture, and cook, stirring, until the beans reduce to a thick mixture; the beans will darken as they cook. Continue adding the mixture, a ladleful at a time, stirring and reducing the liquid before adding the next ladleful. You should end up with a thick purée.

❹ If using cheese, sprinkle it over the beans and cover until the heat in the pan melts the cheese. Alternatively, place under a preheated grill to melt the cheese. Serve at once.

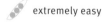 extremely easy

 serves 4

 5–10 minutes, plus 8 hours to soak

 3 hours

Black Bean Nachos

INGREDIENTS

225 g/8 oz dried black
   beans, or canned
   black beans, drained
175–225 g/6–8 oz grated
   cheese, such as
   Cheddar, Fontina,
   pecorino, asiago,
   or a combination
about ¼ tsp cumin seeds
   or ground cumin
about 4 tbsp soured
   cream
pickled jalapeños, sliced
   thinly (optional)
1 tbsp chopped fresh
   coriander
handful of shredded
   lettuce
tortilla chips, to serve

❶ If using dried black beans, soak the beans overnight, then drain. Put in a pan, cover with water and bring to the boil. Boil for 10 minutes, then reduce the heat and simmer for about 1½ hours, or until tender. Drain well.

❷ Spread the beans in a shallow ovenproof dish, then scatter the cheese over the top. Sprinkle with cumin, to taste.

❸ Bake in a preheated oven at 190°C/375°F/Gas Mark 5 for 10–15 minutes, or until the beans are cooked through and the cheese is bubbling and melted.

❹ Remove the beans and cheese from the oven and spoon the soured cream on top. Add the jalapeños, if using, and sprinkle with fresh coriander and lettuce.

❺ Arrange the tortilla chips around the beans, sticking them into the mixture. Serve the nachos at once.

 extremely easy

 serves 4

 5–10 minutes,
plus 8 hours
to soak

 2 hours

Potatoes with Goat's Cheese & Chipotle Cream

INGREDIENTS

1.25 kg/2 lb 12 oz baking
potatoes, peeled and
cut into chunks
pinch of salt
pinch of sugar
200 ml/7 fl oz crème
fraîche
125 ml/4 fl oz vegetable
stock
3 garlic cloves, chopped
finely
a few shakes of bottled
chipotle salsa, or
½ dried chipotle,
reconstituted,
deseeded and sliced
thinly
225 g/8 oz goat's cheese,
sliced
175 g/6 oz mozzarella or
Cheddar cheese,
grated
50 g/1¾ oz Parmesan
or pecorino cheese,
grated
salt

❶ Put the potatoes in a pan of water with the salt and sugar. Bring to the boil and cook for about 10 minutes, or until they are half cooked.

❷ Combine the crème fraîche with the stock, garlic and the chipotle salsa.

❸ Arrange half the potatoes in a casserole. Pour half the crème fraîche sauce over the potatoes and cover with the goat's cheese. Top with the remaining potatoes and the sauce.

❹ Sprinkle with the grated mozzarella or Cheddar cheese, then with either the grated Parmesan or pecorino.

❺ Bake in a preheated oven at 180°C/350°F/Gas Mark 4, or until the potatoes are tender and the cheese topping is lightly golden and crisped in places. Serve at once.

 extremely easy

 serves 4

 15 minutes

 20 minutes

Vegetable Tostadas

INGREDIENTS

vegetable oil, for frying
4 corn tortillas
2–3 tbsp extra-virgin
   olive oil or
   vegetable oil
2 potatoes, diced
1 carrot, diced
3 garlic cloves, chopped
   finely
1 red pepper, deseeded
   and diced
1 tsp mild chilli powder
1 tsp paprika
½ tsp ground cumin
3–4 ripe tomatoes, diced
115 g/4 oz green beans,
   blanched and cut into
   bite-sized lengths
several large pinches
   dried oregano
400 g/14 oz cooked black
   beans, drained
225 g/8 oz crumbled feta
   cheese
3–4 leaves cos lettuce,
   shredded
3–4 spring onions, sliced
   thinly

❶ To make tostadas, fry the tortillas in a small amount of oil in a non-stick pan until crisp.

❷ Heat the olive oil in a frying pan, add the potatoes and carrot, and cook until softened. Add the garlic, red pepper, chilli powder, paprika and cumin. Cook for 2–3 minutes, or until the peppers have softened.

❸ Add the tomatoes, green beans and oregano. Cook for 8–10 minutes, or until the vegetables are tender and form a saucelike mixture. The mixture should not be too dry; add a little water if necessary, to keep it moist.

❹ Heat the black beans in a pan with a tiny amount of water, and keep warm. Reheat the tostadas under the grill.

❺ Layer the beans over the hot tostadas, then sprinkle with the cheese and top with a few spoonfuls of the hot vegetables in sauce. Serve at once, each tostada sprinkled with the lettuce and spring onions.

 very easy

 serves 4

 15 minutes

 20 minutes

Red Rice Pilaf with Roasted Vegetables

125 ml/4 fl oz olive oil
grated rind and juice of
   1 orange
2 tbsp balsamic vinegar
2 tsp coriander seeds
1 bay leaf
½ tsp dried chillies
8–10 small raw
   beetroots, halved
250 g/9 oz shallots
6–8 baby parsnips
4–6 baby carrots
1 tsp chopped fresh
   rosemary leaves
400 g/14 oz red rice
850 ml/1½ pints stock
1 red onion
1 small carrot, cut into
   matchstick strips
1 leek, cut into rounds
85 g/3 oz pine kernels,
   lightly roasted
1 tsp light brown sugar
· 150 g/5½ oz dried
   cranberries, soaked in
   boiling water
1–2 tbsp fresh coriander
salt and pepper

TO SERVE
225 ml/8 fl oz sour cream
2 tbsp chopped roasted
   walnuts

❶ Put about 4 tablespoons of the olive oil in a large bowl and whisk in the orange rind and juice, vinegar and bay leaves. Crush the coriander seeds and chillies lightly, and whisk them in. Trim the beetroots, shallots, parsnips and carrots, add them to the bowl, and stir to coat well.

❷ Turn into a roasting tin and roast in a preheated oven at 200°C/400°F/Gas Mark 6 for 45–55 minutes, turning occasionally. Remove from the oven, sprinkle with the chopped rosemary and salt and pepper, and keep warm.

❸ Put the rice in a large saucepan with the hot stock. Place over a medium-high heat and bring to the boil; reduce the heat to low and simmer, covered, for about 40 minutes, or until the rice is tender and the stock absorbed. Remove from the heat, but do not uncover.

❹ Heat the remaining oil in a large pan. Add the onion and carrot strips and cook for 8–10 minutes, or until tender. Add the leek, pine kernels, and brown sugar, chop the coriander and add it, and cook for 2–3 minutes or until the vegetables are lightly caramelized. Drain the cranberries and stir into the vegetable mixture with the rice. Season to taste.

❺ Arrange the vegetables and rice on a plate and top with the cream. Sprinkle with the chopped walnuts and serve.

easy

serves 4

25 minutes

55 minutes

Curried Rice Patties with Tahini Dressing

INGREDIENTS

½ tsp salt
70 g/2½ oz basmati rice
2 tbsp olive oil
1 red onion, chopped
2 garlic cloves
2 tsp curry powder
½ tsp dried chilli flakes
1 small red pepper,
    deseeded and diced
115 g/4 oz frozen peas
1 small leek, chopped
1 ripe tomato, skinned,
    deseeded, chopped
310 g/11 oz canned
    chickpeas
85 g/3 oz fresh white
    breadcrumbs
1–2 tbsp fresh coriander
1 egg, lightly beaten
vegetable oil, for frying
salt and pepper
cucumber, to garnish
lime wedges, to serve

DRESSING
125 ml/4 fl oz tahini
2 garlic cloves, crushed
½ tsp ground cumin
pinch of cayenne pepper
5 tbsp lemon juice
drizzle of extra-virgin
    olive oil
125 ml/4 fl oz water

❶ To make the dressing, blend the tahini, garlic, cumin, cayenne and lemon juice in a food processor until creamy. Slowly pour in the oil, then gradually add water to make a creamy dressing.

❷ Bring a saucepan of water to the boil. Add the salt and sprinkle in the rice; simmer for 15–20 minutes, or until the rice is just tender. Drain, rinse and set aside.

❸ Heat the olive oil in a large pan. Add the onion and garlic and cook until beginning to soften. Crush the chilli flakes, stir them in with the curry powder, and cook for 2 minutes. Add the pepper, defrosted peas, leek and tomato, and cook gently for 7 minutes, or until tender. Set aside.

❹ Rinse and drain the chickpeas, and process them in the food processor until smooth. Add half the vegetables and process again. Transfer to a large bowl and add the remaining vegetable mixture and breadcrumbs, chop the coriander and add it, and the egg, and mix well. Stir in the rice and season. Chill for 1 hour, then shape into 4–6 patties.

❺ Fry the patties in oil for 6–8 minutes, or until golden. Garnish with cucumber slices and serve with the dressing and lime wedges.

easy

serves 4

20 minutes

40 minutes, plus
1 hour to chill

Spicy Potato & Rice Pilaf

200 g/7 oz basmati rice,
soaked in cold water
for 20 minutes
2 tbsp vegetable oil
½–¾ tsp cumin seeds
225 g/8 oz potatoes, cut
into 1 cm/½ inch
pieces
225 g/8 oz frozen peas,
defrosted
1 green chilli, deseeded
and sliced thinly
(optional)
½ tsp salt
1 tsp garam masala
½ tsp ground turmeric
¼ tsp cayenne pepper
600 ml/1 pint water
2 tbsp chopped fresh
coriander
1 red onion, chopped
finely
natural yogurt, to serve

❶ Rinse the soaked rice under cold running water until the water runs clear. Drain and set aside.

❷ Heat the oil in a large heavy-based saucepan over a medium-high heat. Add the cumin seeds and stir for about 10 seconds, or until the seeds jump and colour.

❸ Add the potatoes, peas and chilli (if using) and stir-fry for 3 minutes, or until the potatoes are beginning to soften.

❹ Add the rice and cook, stirring often, until well coated and beginning to turn translucent. Stir in the salt, garam masala, turmeric and cayenne pepper, then add the water. Bring to the boil, stirring occasionally, then reduce the heat to medium and simmer, covered, until most of the water is absorbed and steam holes cover the surface. Do not stir.

❺ Reduce the heat to very low and, if possible, raise the pan about 2.5 cm/1 inch above the heat source by resting it on a ring. Cover and steam for about 10 minutes longer. Remove from the heat, uncover, cover the rice with kitchen paper, or a clean tea towel, then re-cover the pan. Leave to stand for 5 minutes.

❻ Put the mixture in a bowl and sprinkle with the coriander and onion. Serve hot with yogurt handed round separately.

 very easy

serves 4

10 minutes, plus 20 minutes to soak

35 minutes

Wild Rocket & Tomato Risotto with Mozzarella

INGREDIENTS

2 tbsp olive oil
25 g/1 oz unsalted butter
1 large onion, chopped
  finely
2 garlic cloves, chopped
  finely
350 g/12 oz arborio rice
125 ml/4 fl oz dry white
  vermouth (optional)
1.5 litres/2¾ pints
  vegetable stock,
  simmering
6 vine-ripened or Italian
  plum tomatoes,
  deseeded and
  chopped
125 g/4½ oz wild rocket
handful of fresh basil
  leaves
115 g/4 oz freshly grated
  Parmesan cheese
225 g/8 oz fresh Italian
  buffalo mozzarella,
  grated roughly, or
  diced
salt and pepper

❶ Heat the oil and half the butter in a large frying pan. Add the onion and cook for about 2 minutes, or until the onion just begins to soften. Stir in the garlic and rice, and cook, stirring frequently, until the rice is translucent and well coated with the butter and garlic.

❷ Pour in the white vermouth, if using; it will bubble and steam rapidly and evaporate almost immediately. Add a ladleful (about 225 ml/8 fl oz) of the simmering stock and cook, stirring constantly, until it is absorbed.

❸ Continue adding the stock, about half a ladleful at a time, allowing each addition to be absorbed before adding the next – never allow the rice to dry out while cooking.

❹ Just before the rice is tender, stir in the chopped tomatoes and rocket. Shred the basil leaves and stir them into the risotto immediately. Continue to cook, adding more stock, until the risotto is creamy and the rice is tender but firm to the bite.

❺ Remove from the heat and stir in the remaining butter, and the Parmesan and mozzarella. Season to taste with salt and pepper. Cover, and stand for about 1 minute. Serve immediately, before the mozzarella melts completely.

 very easy

 serves 4

15 minutes

35 minutes

Cheese-topped Risotto Tart with Spinach

INGREDIENTS

185 g/6½ oz plain flour
½ tsp salt
1 tsp caster sugar
115 g/4 oz unsalted
    butter, diced
1 egg yolk, beaten with
    2 tbsp iced water

FILLING
1 quantity basic cooked
    risotto, still warm
    (follow recipe on
    page 62, omitting
    tomatoes, rocket,
    basil and mozzarella)
250 g/9 oz spinach,
    cooked, drained very
    well and chopped
2 tbsp double cream
225 g/8 oz mozzarella,
    preferably buffalo
85 g/3 oz freshly grated
    Parmesan cheese

❶ To make the pastry, sift the flour, salt and sugar into a large bowl and sprinkle the butter over the top. Rub the butter into the flour until the mixture forms coarse crumbs. Sprinkle in the egg mixture and stir to make a dough.

❷ Gather the dough into a ball, wrap it in clingfilm, and chill it for at least 1 hour.

❸ Gently roll out the pastry to a thickness of about 3 mm/ ⅛ inch, then use to line a lightly greased 23–25 cm/ 9–10 inch tart tin with a removable base. Prick the bottom with a fork and chill for 1 hour.

❹ Cover the tart case with baking paper and fill with baking beans. Bake blind in a preheated oven at 200°C/400°F/ Gas Mark 6 for about 20 minutes, or until edge of the pastry is golden. Remove the beans and paper and set aside. Reduce the oven temperature to 180°C/350°F/Gas Mark 4.

❺ Put the risotto in a bowl and stir in the spinach, cream, half the mozzarella and half the Parmesan cheeses. Spoon it into the tart case and smooth it over. Sprinkle the remaining cheeses on top.

❻ Bake for 12–15 minutes, or until cooked through and golden. Cool slightly on a wire rack, then serve warm.

 easy

 serves 4

 20 minutes, plus 1 hour to chill

 35 minutes

Salads & Side Dishes

A recipe that will change the image of lentils, often accused of being boring and a staple food of cranks, is Lentils Simmered with Fruit. Apples, pineapples, tomatoes and even bananas go into this intriguing dish, which is spiced up with cayenne pepper. And if you have never liked broad beans, you may be surprised by Broad Beans with Feta & Lemon – tossed in a delicious olive oil and lemon dressing with fresh dill.

Thai-style Carrot & Mango Salad

INGREDIENTS

4 carrots
1 small, ripe mango
200 g/7 oz firm tofu
1 tbsp fresh chives,
   chopped

DRESSING
2 tbsp orange juice
1 tbsp lime juice
1 tsp clear honey
½ tsp orange-flower
   water
1 tsp sesame oil
1 tsp sesame seeds,
   toasted

❶ Peel the carrots and grate them roughly. Peel and stone the mango and slice it thinly.

❷ Cut the tofu into 1 cm/½ inch dice-shaped pieces and toss together with the carrots and mango in a wide salad bowl.

❸ For the dressing, place all the ingredients in a screw-top jar and shake well to mix evenly.

❹ Pour the dressing over the salad and toss well to coat the salad evenly.

❺ Just before serving, toss the salad lightly and sprinkle with chives. Serve immediately.

 extremely easy

 serves 4

10 minutes

0 minutes

Rice with Black Beans

INGREDIENTS

1 onion, chopped
5 garlic cloves, chopped
225 ml/8 fl oz vegetable
   stock
2 tbsp vegetable oil
175 g/6 oz long-grain
   rice
½ tsp ground cumin
225 ml/8 fl oz liquid from
   cooking black beans
   (including some black
   beans)
salt and pepper

TO GARNISH
3–5 spring onions,
   sliced thinly
2 tbsp chopped fresh
   coriander leaves

❶ Put the onion in a blender with the garlic and stock, and blend until it is the consistency of a chunky sauce.

❷ Heat the oil in a heavy-based pan and cook the rice until it is golden. Add the onion mixture, with the cooking liquid from the black beans (and any beans floating in it). Add the cumin, with salt and pepper to taste.

❸ Cover the pan and cook over a medium-low heat for about 10 minutes, or until the rice is just tender. The rice should be evenly coloured by the black bean liquid.

❹ Fluff up the rice with a fork, and leave to rest for about 5 minutes, covered. Serve sprinkled with spring onions sliced thinly, and chopped coriander.

 extremely easy

 serves 4

 10 minutes

 15 minutes, plus
5 minutes to stand

Lentils Simmered with Fruit

INGREDIENTS

125 g/4½ oz brown or
green lentils
about 1 litre/1¾ pints
water
2 tbsp vegetable oil
3 small to medium
onions, chopped
4 garlic cloves, roughly
chopped
1 large tart apple,
roughly chopped
about ¼ ripe pineapple,
skin removed and
roughly chopped
2 tomatoes, deseeded
and diced
1 almost ripe banana, cut
into bite-sized pieces
salt
cayenne pepper, to taste
fresh parsley sprig, to
garnish

❶ Combine the lentils with the water in a pan, then bring to the boil. Reduce the heat and simmer over a low heat for about 40 minutes, or until the lentils are tender. Do not let them get mushy.

❷ Meanwhile, heat the oil in a frying pan and fry the onions and garlic until lightly browned and softened. Add the apple and continue to cook until golden. Add the pineapple, heat through, stirring, then add the tomatoes. Cook over a medium heat until thickened, stirring occasionally.

❸ Drain the lentils, reserving 125 ml/4 fl oz of the cooking liquid. Add the drained lentils to the sauce, stirring in the reserved liquid if necessary. Heat through for a minute to mingle the flavours.

❹ Add the banana to the pan, then season with salt and cayenne pepper. Serve garnished with parsley.

 very easy

 serves 4

 25 minutes

 1 hour
20 minutes

Gazpacho Rice Salad

INGREDIENTS

extra-virgin olive oil
1 onion, chopped finely
4 garlic cloves, chopped finely
200 g/7 oz long-grain white rice or basmati
350 ml/12 fl oz vegetable stock or water
1½ tsp dried thyme
3 tbsp sherry vinegar
1 tsp Dijon mustard
1 tsp honey or sugar
1 red pepper, deseeded and chopped
½ yellow pepper, deseeded and chopped
½ green pepper, deseeded and chopped
1 red onion, chopped
½ cucumber, peeled, deseeded and chopped (optional)
3 tomatoes, deseeded and chopped
2–3 tbsp chopped flat-leaved parsley
salt and pepper

TO SERVE
12 cherry tomatoes
12 black olives, stoned
1 tbsp flaked almonds, toasted

 very easy

 serves 4

 25 minutes

55 minutes, plus 30 minutes to stand

❶ Heat 2 tablespoons of the oil in a large saucepan. Add the onion and cook for 2 minutes, stirring frequently, until it begins to soften. Stir in half the garlic and cook for a further minute.

❷ Add the rice, stirring to coat, and cook for 2 minutes or until translucent. Stir in the stock and half the thyme, and bring to the boil; season with salt and pepper. Simmer very gently, covered, for about 20 minutes or until tender. Stand, covered, for 15 minutes, then uncover and leave to cool.

❸ Whisk the vinegar with the remaining garlic and thyme, the mustard, honey and salt and pepper in a large bowl. Slowly whisk in about 80 ml/3 fl oz of the olive oil. Using a fork, fluff the rice into the vinaigrette.

❹ Add the peppers, red onion, cucumber, tomatoes and parsley. Toss and season.

❺ Transfer to a serving bowl, then halve the cherry tomatoes and chop the olives roughly, and sprinkle over the salad with the almonds to garnish.

Coconut-scented Brown Rice

INGREDIENTS

350 ml/12 fl oz water
225 ml/8 fl oz coconut
    milk
1 tsp salt
200 g/7 oz long-grain
    brown rice
1 lemon
1 cinnamon stick
about 15 whole cloves
1 tbsp chopped fresh
    parsley
fresh coconut shavings
    (optional)

❶ Bring the water to the boil in a heavy-based saucepan and whisk in the coconut milk. Return the liquid to the boil, add the salt and sprinkle in the rice.

❷ Pare 2–3 strips of lemon rind and add to the saucepan with the cinnamon stick and the cloves.

❸ Reduce the heat to low, cover and simmer gently for about 45 minutes, or until the rice is tender and the liquid is completely absorbed. Uncover and leave the rice over high heat for about 1 minute, to allow any steam to escape and the rice to dry out a little.

❹ Remove the cloves, if wished, then sprinkle with the herbs and coconut, if using; fork into a warmed serving bowl and serve.

extremely easy

serves 4

5 minutes

1 hour

COOK'S TIP
This technique can be used to cook white rice as well, but the fuller flavour of brown rice works well with the warm flavour of the spices.

Broad Beans with Feta & Lemon

INGREDIENTS

500 g/1 lb 2 oz peeled
    broad beans
4 tbsp extra-virgin
    olive oil
1 tbsp lemon juice
1 tbsp chopped finely
    fresh dill, plus a little
    extra for garnishing
60 g/2¼ oz feta cheese,
    drained and diced
salt and pepper
lemon wedges, to serve

❶ Bring a saucepan of water to the boil. Add the broad beans and cook them for about 2 minutes, or until tender. Drain well.

❷ When the beans are cool enough to handle, remove and discard the outer skins to reveal the bright green beans underneath (see Cook's Tip). Put the peeled beans in a serving bowl.

❸ Stir together the olive oil and lemon juice, then season with salt and pepper to taste. Pour the dressing over the warm beans, add the dill, and stir the beans. Adjust the seasoning if necessary.

❹ If serving hot, toss with the feta cheese and sprinkle with extra dill. Alternatively, leave to cool and chill until required. Remove from the refrigerator 10 minutes before serving, season, then sprinkle with the feta and extra dill. Serve with lemon wedges.

 very easy

 serves 4

 10–15 minutes

 10 minutes

COOK'S TIP

If you are lucky enough to have very young broad beans at the start of the season, it isn't necessary to remove the outer skin.

Green Tabbouleh

INGREDIENTS

300 g/10½ oz bulgar
    wheat
200 g/7 oz cucumber
6 spring onions
15 g/½ oz fresh flat-
    leaved parsley
1 unwaxed lemon
about 2 tbsp garlic-
    flavoured olive oil
salt and pepper

❶ Bring a kettle of water to the boil. Place the bulgar wheat in a heatproof bowl, pour over 600 ml/1 pint boiling water and cover. Set aside for at least 20 minutes, until the wheat absorbs the water and becomes tender.

❷ Meanwhile, cut the cucumber in half lengthways, then cut each half into 3 strips lengthways. Using a teaspoon, scoop out and discard the seeds. Chop the cucumber strips into bite-sized pieces and put in a serving bowl.

❸ Trim the top of the green parts of each of the spring onions, then cut each in half lengthways. Chop finely and add to the cucumber.

❹ Place the parsley on a chopping board, sprinkle with salt, and chop the leaves and stalks very finely. Add to the cucumber and onions. Grate the lemon rind into the bowl.

❺ When the bulgar wheat is cool, squeeze out excess water with your hands or by pressing it through a sieve, then add to the other ingredients.

❻ Cut the lemon in half and squeeze the juice of one half over the salad. Add 2 tablespoons of the garlic-flavoured oil and stir all the ingredients. Season to taste and add extra lemon juice or oil if needed. Cover and chill until required.

very easy

serves 4

20 minutes,
plus 20 minutes
to soak

0 minutes

Courgettes & Tomatoes with Green Chilli Vinaigrette

❶ Roast the mild chilli, or the combination of the green pepper and chilli, in a heavy-based ungreased frying pan or under a preheated grill until the skin is charred. Place in a plastic bag, twist to seal well, and leave the mixture to stand for 20 minutes.

❷ Peel the skin from the chilli and pepper, if using, then remove the seeds and slice the flesh. Set aside.

❸ Bring about 5 cm/2 inches water to the boil in the bottom of a steamer. Add the courgettes to the top part of the steamer, cover and steam for about 5 minutes, or until just tender.

❹ Meanwhile, combine the garlic, sugar, cumin, vinegar, olive oil and coriander thoroughly in a bowl. Stir in the chilli and pepper (if using), then season with salt and pepper to taste.

❺ Arrange the courgettes and tomatoes in a serving bowl or on a plate and spoon the chilli dressing over it. Toss gently and serve.

 very easy

 serves 4

 15 minutes, plus 20 minutes to stand

 10 minutes

Desserts

Vegetarians love puddings as much as everyone else. However, they may be more inclined to use quality unrefined and organic ingredients, which are now widely available, which give the best results. The best chocolate, which has a high proportion of cocoa solids, will produce a better Saucy Chocolate Pudding than cheap cooking chocolate, while a pale golden, unrefined caster sugar will add a special flavour and character to the Lemon & Lime Syllabub. The recipes in the following pages use milk and cream, nuts and berries to create imaginative desserts.

Almond Rice Custard

INGREDIENTS

*85 g/3 oz whole
  blanched almonds*
1 litre/1¾ pints milk
25 g/1 oz rice flour
pinch of salt
60 g/2¼ oz sugar
*½ tsp almond essence or
  1 tbsp almond-flavour
  liqueur*
*toasted flaked almonds,
  to decorate*

TO SERVE (OPTIONAL)
*350 g/12 oz fresh
  strawberries, sliced,
  sprinkled with 2 tbsp
  sugar and chilled*

❶ Put the almonds in a food processor and process until a thick paste forms. Bring 225 ml/8 fl oz of the milk to the boil. Gradually pour into the almond paste, with the machine running, until the mixture is smooth. Leave to stand for about 10 minutes.

❷ Combine the rice flour, salt and sugar in a large bowl, then stir in about 4–5 tablespoons of the milk to form a smooth paste.

❸ Bring the remaining milk to the boil in a saucepan. Pour the hot milk into the rice flour paste and stir constantly, then return the mixture to the saucepan and bring to the boil. Reduce the heat and simmer for about 10 minutes, or until smooth and thickened. Remove from the heat.

❹ Strain the almond milk through a very fine sieve into the simmering rice custard, pressing through the almonds with the back of a spoon. Return to the heat and simmer for 7–10 minutes, or until it becomes thick.

❺ Remove from the heat and stir in the almond essence. Cool slightly, stirring, then pour into individual bowls. Sprinkle with the almonds and serve with the strawberries, if wished. The custard may be chilled to serve later. It will thicken as it cools.

 very easy

 serves 4

 15 minutes, plus 10 minutes to stand

 30 minutes

Saucy Chocolate Pudding

300 ml/10 fl oz milk
75 g/2¾ oz semisweet
* chocolate*
½ tsp vanilla essence
100 g/3½ oz caster sugar
100 g/3½ oz butter
150 g/5½ oz self-raising
* flour*
2 tbsp cocoa powder
icing sugar, to dust

SAUCE
3 tbsp cocoa powder
50 g/1¾ oz light
* muscovado sugar*
300 ml/10 fl oz boiling
* water*

❶ Grease an 850 ml/1½ pint ovenproof dish lightly.

❷ Place the milk in a small pan. Break the chocolate into pieces and add to the milk. Heat gently, stirring until the chocolate melts. Leave to cool slightly. Stir in the vanilla essence.

❸ Beat together the caster sugar and butter in a bowl until light and fluffy. Strain the flour and cocoa powder together. Add to the bowl with the chocolate milk and beat until smooth, using an electric whisk if you have one. Pour the mixture into the prepared dish.

❹ To make the sauce, mix together the cocoa powder and sugar. Add a little boiling water and mix to a smooth paste, then stir in the remaining water. Pour the sauce over the pudding, but do not mix in.

❺ Place the dish on a baking tray and bake in a preheated oven, 180°C/350°F/Gas Mark 4, for 40 minutes, or until dry on top and springy to the touch. Leave to stand for about 5 minutes, then dust with a little icing sugar before serving.

 very easy

 serves 4

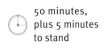 15 minutes

50 minutes, plus 5 minutes to stand

Chocolate Hazelnut Pots

2 eggs
2 egg yolks
15 g/½ oz caster sugar
1 tsp cornflour
600 ml/1 pint milk
85 g/3 oz dark chocolate
4 tbsp chocolate and
   hazelnut spread

TO DECORATE
grated chocolate or large
   chocolate curls

very easy

serves 4

15 minutes

55 minutes

❶ Beat together the eggs, egg yolks, caster sugar and cornflour until well combined. Heat the milk until almost boiling.

❷ Gradually pour the milk onto the eggs, whisking as you do so. Melt the chocolate with the chocolate and hazelnut spread in a bowl set over a pan of gently simmering water, then whisk the melted chocolate mixture into the eggs.

❸ Pour into 6 small ovenproof dishes and cover the dishes with foil. Place them in a roasting tin. Fill the tin with boiling water to come halfway up the sides of the dishes.

❹ Bake in a preheated oven, 160°C/325°F/Gas Mark 3, for 35–40 minutes, or until the custard is just set. Remove from the tin and cool, then chill until required. Serve decorated with grated chocolate or chocolate curls.

COOK'S TIP
This dish is traditionally made in little pots called pots de crème, which are individual ovenproof dishes with a lid. Ramekins are fine. The dessert can also be made in one large dish; cook for about 1 hour or until set.

Berry Cheesecake

INGREDIENTS

BASE
75 g/2¾ oz vegetarian
 margarine
175 g/6 oz oatmeal
 biscuits
50 g/1¾ oz desiccated
 coconut

TOPPING
1½ tsp gelozone
9 tbsp cold water
125 ml/4 fl oz evaporated
 milk
1 egg
6 tbsp light brown sugar
450 g/1 lb soft cream
 cheese
350 g/12 oz mixed
 berries
2 tbsp clear honey

very easy

serves 4

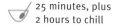

25 minutes, plus
2 hours to chill

10 minutes

❶ Put the margarine in a saucepan and heat until melted. Put the biscuits in a food processor and blend until smooth or crush finely with a rolling pin. Stir into the margarine with the coconut.

❷ Press the mixture into a base-lined 20 cm/8 inch spring-form tin, and chill while preparing the filling.

❸ To make the topping, sprinkle the gelozone over the water and stir to dissolve. Bring to the boil and boil for 2 minutes. Leave to cool slightly.

❹ Put the milk, egg, sugar and soft cream cheese in a bowl and beat until smooth. Stir in 50 g/1¾ oz of the berries. Stir in the gelozone in a stream, stirring constantly, until fully incorporated.

❺ Spoon the mixture onto the biscuit base and return to the refrigerator for 2 hours, or until set.

❻ Remove the cheesecake from the tin and transfer to a serving plate. Arrange the remaining berries on top of the cheesecake and drizzle the honey over the top. Serve.

COOK'S TIP
Warm the honey slightly to make it runnier and easier to drizzle.

Lemon & Lime Syllabub

*50 g/1¾ oz caster sugar
grated rind and juice of
  1 small lemon
grated rind and juice of
  1 small lime
50 ml/2 fl oz Marsala or
  medium sherry
300 ml/10 fl oz double
  cream
lime and lemon rind,
  to decorate*

❶ Put the sugar, fruit juices and rind and sherry in a bowl, mix well, and leave to infuse for 2 hours.

❷ Add the cream to the mixture and whisk until it just holds its shape.

❸ Spoon the mixture into 4 tall serving glasses and chill in the refrigerator for 2 hours.

❹ Decorate with lime and lemon rind, and serve.

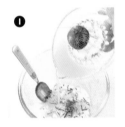  

 extremely easy

 serves 4

 10 minutes,
plus 2 hours
to infuse and
2 hours to chill

0 minutes

COOK'S TIP
Replace the double cream with natural yogurt for a healthier version of this dessert, or use half quantities of both. Whisk the cream before adding it to the yogurt.